Still Your Sweetie Pie

World War II Love Story of
Emil and Ellie Takacs

Compiled by Adele (Takacs) Johnston

Contents taken from one hundred postcards and letters
that Emil wrote to Ellie from 1941-1945
while serving in the United States Coast Guard.

<u>Published by Paper Bridges</u>

December, 2020

Disclaimer:

This is a work of nonfiction, based on postcards and letters written by Emil to Ellie Takacs between 1941-1945.

All names, characters, places and incidents used by the author are attributable to him, and to him alone. Any references to actual people, living, dead (or otherwise incarnate), or to known events or locales has come from the annals of history.

Book and Cover design by MaryLee Marilee
Editing/Proofreading by MaryLee Marilee
Photos from family albums

ISBN: 978-1-7347888-4-6 Print Book

ISBN: 978-1-7347888-5-3 E-Book

Paper Bridges
Books

Paper Bridges
771B, S.R. 97
Linking Author   **Perrysville, OH 44864**   *To Reader*
email: PaperBridgesPublisher@gmail.com

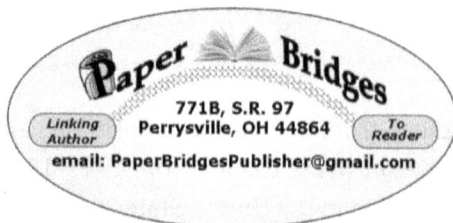

Contents

Prologue

As children, my sister Donna and I used to sneak into the attic and excitedly read the love letters that our dad wrote to our mom when he was in the Coast Guard during World War II. It was such an adventure, because we thought we were doing something mysterious and naughty.

Sadly, our mom passed away in 1998. Dad gave us the letters in 2000. When I received them, I arranged them in chronological order and began reading voraciously. I read them in four sittings—twenty-five letters each night. Even though I knew the ending, it read like an engaging love story with a happily-ever-after ending. I know war isn't romantic, but when you're reading love letters about your parents, you can't deny the romantic element.

In 2001, I decided to begin to write our parents' love story. I took excerpts and direct quotes from each letter. I was able to ask Dad questions, and he would explain and embellish with more stories. His memory was remarkable. How I wish Mom were here to have her input, and how I wish we had her letters to Dad. However, they were lost at sea. A sailor had nowhere to keep such things while going from port to port.

I have dedicated the book to our parents, of course, but also to my sister Donna (Takacs) Amstutz, who was always the more romantic sibling.

The title of the book was obvious from the start...
Still Your Sweetie Pie... the endearing closing to every letter.
It was written in our dad's beautiful handwriting.

What a privilege we have had to experience this glimpse into our parents' courtship and beginning of their marriage during those difficult war years. What a wonderful legacy of love they left my sister and me!

Written with love by Adele (Takacs) Johnston

Meeting on the Street Car

Emil was 20 years old, of slim build, standing tall at five feet, eight inches. He displayed a healthy head of wavy, brown hair and warm, brown eyes that were touched with a little mischief.

While riding the local streetcar on his way to work at Alcoa, those eyes scanned the crowd and settled on a slender, attractive, raven-haired beauty who was standing in the aisle near him.

"Hmmm, quite pretty" considered Emil. *"I probably should give her my seat, but I'm worried she might think I was too forward. I think I'll just sneak a few glances at her when I think she's not looking."*

Ellie was also 20 years old and was also riding to work. She noticed the handsome guy sitting nearby and saw him sneaking quick glances at her.

"Hmmm, why doesn't he give me his seat?" she questioned silently. *"Probably too stuck up, or maybe too shy,"* she pondered. *"I do love that thick, wavy hair of his. Well, I'll just have to admire him from afar, because it certainly would not be lady-like for me to speak to him first,"* she rationalized.

The second day they were both traveling to work, Emil got the nerve to speak to Ellie. He did so in spite of being very nervous, because he really thought she was so pretty and wholesome looking, and those dreamy blue eyes just "knocked him for a loop!"

"So," Emil commented, "I've noticed you lately. Can I ask where you work?"

"I'm a comptometer operator at Kaynee Company."

"How long have you worked there?"

"About a year," Ellie stated.

"Boy, this is going to be difficult to get to know her at this rate," Emil complained to himself.

Ellie got off at her stop before Emil could question her more. But he noticed that she did glance back at him before she departed. That gave Emil the glimmer of hope he needed to pursue the conversation the next day.

Now it's the third day they rode together, and a little kind of familiarity had settled in. Emil was again seated when she boarded, and this time he didn't hesitate to offer her his seat. As she slowly walked toward him, he gallantly got up and gestured with a sweep of his arm for her to sit down. She politely accepted. Emil couldn't help but notice her lovely scent as she slipped past him and that stylish, wavy dark hair was certainly appealing.

"So, since I gave you my seat, maybe we should know each other's names," Emil stated. "I'm Emil Takacs."

Ellie quietly responded, "I'm Eldrid Lohman."

"So where do you live?" Emil inquired bravely.

"On Memphis Avenue by Old Brookie."

"Boy, I really want to ask her out," Emil thought. So Emil mustered up all of his courage, at the risk of being refused, and blurted out, "So, I was wondering if you would like to go to the movies with me sometime. We'd have to walk, because I don't have a car, but my brother Bill does, but I'm not sure he'd let me borrow it," he rambled. "So, how about it?"

Ellie listened patiently while a few butterflies fluttered in her stomach. With a slight smile and a little giggle, she quietly responded, "Sure, I like movies."

With a relieved sigh, Emil asked if this Friday was good. She nodded her head in agreement.

Still Your Sweetie Pie

And so began their journey of love, as they made plans for their very first date. Little did they know that they would travel through life together, which included World War II, for FIFTY-FIVE YEARS!

Chapter One

The month was August. The year was 1940. The place was Cleveland, Ohio. They were both twenty years old when they met on the streetcar. He worked for Alcoa as an inspector of aluminum aircraft cylinder heads. She worked at Kaynee Company as a comptometer operator. He was attracted to her because of her good, wholesome looks. She was standing and he was sitting the first time he talked to her, and he didn't even give up his seat!

They joked about that in years to come. But it didn't matter, because she went out with him after the third time he talked to her and asked her for a date. They walked to the Memphis movie theatre. Thereafter, he used his brother Bill's 1935 Ford for their dates. The only problem was that he had to take his brother to work before the date and pick him up after the date. That didn't cramp his style, though, because Emil knew after the first date that he wanted to marry Ellie.

The romance blossomed, and then the United States entered World War II after Pearl Harbor was bombed by the Japanese on December 7, 1941. The next day, Emil joined the Coast Guard feeling very proud to serve his country in the war effort, but very disturbed that the Japs dared to bomb us. He decided on the Coast Guard because he didn't want to be in the infantry, and he heard they served better food. That proved to be true. He didn't tell anyone about his enlistment until it was all said and done. One can only imagine everyone's reaction. Things moved quickly after that, as only a short ten days later he was deployed to St. Louis, Missouri, which began a four-year journey through the difficult wartimes ahead.

December 18, 1941 was the date of the first correspondence that Emil Rupert Takacs sent to his sweetheart, Eldrid June Lohman. The following story is their love story etched in the one hundred letters that Emil wrote to Ellie while he traveled the world in the pursuit of peace. We do not know what happened to the letters that Ellie wrote to Emil. We can only assume that they were read over and over again, and then lost at sea when the war was over. A traveling serviceman couldn't carry much in his duffle bag.

Postcard number one—December 18, 1941, St. Louis, Missouri:

"So far everything has been wonderful," Emil writes. *"These fellows are certainly swell to me. They also left their honeys behind."*

Postcard number two—December 29, 1941, New Orleans, LA (boot camp, Algiers, LA):

"Boy they didn't waste any time in getting us busy... please write soon and send me a snapshot of you... I miss you an awful lot, but it won't be long."

First airmail letter (which cost 6 cents), postmarked December 29, New Orleans, LA:

"...so excited from just reading your letter that I can hardly think of anything to write. Your picture cheers me up a lot."

Ellie spent that first Christmas they were apart with Emil's family. Emil sent her a watch for Christmas. He asked her if she wanted a ring or watch, and she said she'd rather have a watch, because she figured she'd get the ring eventually. Pretty clever, that Ellie.

Emil's letter continues describing the routine in camp: *"up at 5:45 a.m. to exercise, breakfast at 8 a.m., do drills, marching, life-saving and rifle instruction... rest and lunch... more drills between 1-4 p.m. Study until 8 p.m. after supper... lights out, 9:30 p.m."*

Second airmail letter, sent on January 5, 1942:

"Honey, I would like to hear from you every day... when I don't hear from you I haven't anybody to give me courage. Please understand."

Christmas dinner in camp was turkey and trimmings, ice cream and two kinds of pie. Every Sunday they had fried chicken, which Emil liked, but every Friday was fish, which he didn't like. He said he didn't drink but was back to smoking cigarettes, because they didn't have enough time between meals to enjoy a whole cigar, which he preferred.

Last letter from New Orleans, January 10, 1942:

"Honey, nothing could ever stop me from loving one as sweet as you. Please believe that."

Then Emil described how one guy fell out of a lifeboat because he didn't follow orders. He also mentions that the movies were about the only entertainment that they both could enjoy at camp and at home. Ellie loved the movies. Emil continued to describe life at camp, dividing his time between kitchen and guard duty and detail work.

(The remaining chapters take Emil from the University of Chicago to the ore boat, *The Smith Thompson,* patrolling the Great Lakes, to Boston for electrical school, to San Francisco, to Hawaii, to New Guinea and eventually overseas on the ammunition ship *The USS Murzim.)*

Chapter Two

The next seven letters and postcards were sent from Chicago, where Emil was stationed from January 22, 1942 until April, 1942.

Excerpts from a letter dated January 22, 1942:

"Dearest Honeybunch,

...so wonderful to hear your voice again." (Apparently a phone call was made, which was only three minutes long.) The move to Chicago was a surprise, as they were told at 4 p.m. Tuesday that they were leaving at 4 a.m. Wednesday. Emil felt lucky, because he was closer to home, as other men were sent to Virginia, New York, and Boston. He keeps hoping he will be stationed in the Great Lakes region. Emil said they get to go out every-other night from six to midnight, and that the food here is *"second to home cooking."*

He closes the letter affectionately:

"Always your honey..."

January 28, 1942:

"Hello Sweet..."

Emil went to the Chicago Museum. *"...never in my life saw a building so beautiful..."* He said he'd put in a request for a weekend liberty but doesn't know where to go, because it's only thirty-six hours, and he can't come home.

"One of these days when we are married, we are going to take a special trip to Chicago to visit the museum alone."

He was appointed temporary platoon leader and petty officer of the guard. And now his letters include the shorthand for "I love you," that Ellie used to write to him.

"Always your honey..."

January 29, 1942:

"Hello darling. I'm making history writing four letters in four days." Letters used to get bunched up, so he was experimenting as to whether regular or airmail delivery was best. He also had his first swimming lesson. Ellie must have injured her ankle, because Emil asked how it was.

"Have you missed me much, darling? I know you have. Now don't go thinking that I'm conceited because I know I am being so."

This is the time Emil also got the nickname, "Tacky." He talks about the wonderful life they could have together.

"Always Your Sweetie Pie..."

February 5, 1942:

This was a postcard of Buckingham Fountain in Grand Park Chicago. The guys were on liberty, and it was sent to Ellie as a joke by a fellow Coast Guard buddy who had looked over Emil's shoulder while he was reading one of Ellie's letters. This is too funny.

"Dearest Sweetie Pie...

...Having a few drinks... have to carry Emil back to duty. P.S. I gave him the kiss."

Guess the guys have to have a little fun now and then.

February 20, 1942:

"My dearest darling..."

Emil was worried because he hadn't gotten a letter for a while. He had a *"sick and empty feeling."* He also thanked Ellie for the stamps she sent and promised he would never be tempted when he went out with the guys who weren't going steady. (I'm sure with all the "Dear John" letters guys got, couples had to constantly reassure each other of their devotion.) Ellie also promised she wouldn't go out with anyone else, either. Emil requested another photo of her. (How important those pictures were.)

"Always Your Sweetie Pie..."

March 3, 1942:

"Dearest Darling..."

Emil had received a large photo of Ellie but was disappointed because she wasn't smiling. (Knowing my mom, she was probably trying to look dramatic and mysterious with that movie-star romantic look.) Anyway, Emil commented that he had received three letters that day and a check. He kidded about going out and getting drunk on the check.

"...good things happening, went to rifle range, got lots of letters and a subscription to Reader's Digest from a friend (which he read till he died).*"*

"Gosh, I miss you so terribly much."

"Always Your Sweetie Pie..."

7

(He couldn't think of anything else to say and still had an empty page, so he filled it with a giant, I LOVE YOU in shorthand.) Cute. (I noticed that the letters were stamped by the post office with BUY DEFENSE SAVINGS BONDS AND STAMPS.)

March 9, 1942:

"Dearest Darling..."

Emil was now the supervisor of five-hundred men and was in charge of writing out schedules, because the fellow who was in charge had left. He mentioned that he received a cigar in the mail. *"...I think I'll walk around with a cigar in my mouth all day."* He also noted that it was snowy and cold and windy.

"Gosh, honey, I can hardly wait till I can buy you the ring. How about a 10-Karat diamond?"

"Always Your Sweetie Pie," and a small shorthand , I LOVE YOU, claiming he was stingy today.

April 9, 1942:

Emil left the University of Chicago and was now in old, or South Chicago and would be shipped out on a lake steamer. His duty was to guard the ship when going through the locks on the Great Lakes. This would take twelve days. Now he could send his letters free of postage.

"I hope you're not angry with me for not writing so often."

"Always Your Sweetie Pie, Emil."

To my honey with love,
Eldred

Chapter Three

There were thirteen letters from the *Smith Thompson* ore ship on the Great Lakes from June 1, 1942-March 20, 1943. I wondered why there were no letters between April 9 and June 21, 1942, and then I realized that Emil was home on leave in May, and he and Ellie got engaged!

June 21, 1942:

"My Dearest Darling..."

The letter began with Emil's explanation that they kept getting shuffled from port to port around the Great Lakes, and he never knew when he was going to be in Cleveland. He had to apologize for not sending Ellie a June 19 birthday card, because he thought he was going to be in Cleveland and be able to wish her Happy Birthday in person. *"...no birthday greeting could justify the most wonderful girl in all the world, and I'm sure lucky to be engaged to this same person."*

"Always Your Sweetie Pie,

"Love, Emil"

August 1, 1942:

"Hello Darlin..."

Emil couldn't tell Ellie his duties because of censorship, but he was writing from Seneca, Illinois. (He was picking up ore in Lake Superior ports and unloading it in the Lake Erie ports. Ellie must have bawled him out for something, and he apologized and promised to be more considerate. He suggested she buy Fred Waring's recording of the Coast Guard song, *"Semper Paratus,"* and *"Coast Guard Forever."* He also mentioned that he hitchhiked to Streater and La Salle, Illinois, which was thirty miles from Seneca. The couple who picked him up invited him for a home-cooked meal.

"Always Your Sweetie Pie,

"Love, Emil"

August 20, 1942:

This letter was sent from the La Salle Hotel on hotel stationery. Rooms cost one dollar a night.

"Hello Darlin..."

Emil sent a locket to niece Barbie. And he requested his tennis shoes and tennis racquet from his sister, Tillie. He wished Ellie could be with him at the hotel. *"...just think of the day when we will register as Mr. and Mrs. PPS: Don't forget the pineapple pie."*

The next nine letters were written on Hotel Berkshire stationery, where the men stayed in Chicago. He was in room 507.

September 25, 1942:

"Hello Darlin..."

Emil was now doing boat patrol on the river. He saw Gary Cooper in "The Pride of the Yankees," and a short with the Andrew Sisters. They patrolled ten hours and got twenty-four off through the week. He mentioned that he bought Ellie

a Coast Guard pin (which I have). *"Darlin, do you miss me?"*
Written in shorthand was "I Love You, and "Miss You."

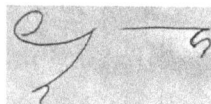

October 14, 1942:

"Dearest Darlin...

Ellie must have wired Emil that she was coming to visit.
He asked when she wanted him to take his leave—at Thanksgiving or Christmas. Ellie must have asked him to tell something exciting that happened on the ship, so he related this
story:

*"I was mopping the deck while on duty one morning and
noticed something in the water. It was a sailor. I grabbed the
body by the collar and hauled him ashore."*

The body had been in the water about two weeks,
according to the morgue, and he was a Navy man. He said it
didn't bother him, because he was able to eat a big breakfast
afterward! (I'll bet Ellie didn't ask for any more stories after
that.) They also started making wedding plans. *"...more
determined than ever to be married a year from this
Thanksgiving,"* wrote Emil.

November 20, 1942:

This letter written after Ellie's visit and began, *"Hello
Sweetness,"* and just had written on the front and back, *"I Love
You Dear,"* and ditto marks all the way down both sides. Emil
also wrote several *"I Love You"* marks in shorthand. Guess
they had a memorable visit!

December 29, 1942:

Emil had been home for Christmas and wrote:

"Hello Dearest,

"Yes, sweet, I got back safe and sound at 7:30 this morning... give my love to everyone and tell Rose and Tillie (his sisters) *I got back O.K."*

His buddy, Jerry, thought he would come back married. *"Won't he be surprised in a few months,"* Emil wrote. (They were planning an April wedding.)

Emil on leave at Christmas, posing with Ellie,
and brother, Bill. 1942.
Taken at his sister and brother-in-law's home
(Rose and Carl Gedeon).

January 9, 1943:

Emil had sent some Christmas photos that Uncle Carl took. His roommate saw them and remarked that Ellie was a beautiful girl. Emil wondered out loud if he would be able to get a lot of rest after they were married, but then he kidded about being more worn out. At dinner that night they had half-a-dozen fried oysters with hot sauce. *"It really hit the spot,"* Emil wrote.

February 2, 1943:

This letter was written from the Stockyards in Chicago.

"Hello Dearest,"

Emil sent two small photos of himself and wrote, *"Don't you dare give them all away. I want you to keep one. OK sweet. …Honey, I miss you so much… I will try to come home the weekend of 21st of February. But don't count on it honey."* (Plans were always so uncertain.)

February 14, 1943:

"My Dearest Valentine,

"How is my honey today? Well sweet, in a few days we will have known each other for two years, and darling, those two years have been the best in my life. You'll never know how much they have meant to me and how wonderful it will be to have you as my wife soon. That's with all my heart, dear."

"Always Your Sweetie Pie,

'Love, Emil"

March 10, 1943:

"Dearest Darlin',

As the wedding date approaches, Emil is sounding anxious and writes: *"The hell with the date, honey, here goes. Before I say anything definite let me know if you will marry me between the 28th of March and the 7th of April... Dearest, I had to read the letter over three times before I realized what you were trying to say, and when I finally did wake up, well, I never felt so happy in all my life."* (Apparently Ellie said YES.)

"Always Your Sweetie Pie,

"Love, Emil"

March 15, 1943:

"My Dearest Future Wife,"

Emil got up the nerve to tell the chief he was getting married, and he asked for leave. The chief said, *"Takacs, why you just had a leave about three months ago, but seeing you're going to get married, it's granted."* He then went on to explain that he could get his leave on March 30th, and they could get blood tests and a marriage license and get married on April 3. After that, he would still have six days leave, and he was still worried about plans getting messed up if he got transferred. But he added, *"Darlin', I'm not going to let anything interfere with our plans."*

He mentions the reaction Ellie's sister, Dorothy, would have to the marriage. *"Well, he finally asked her to marry him!"* (Sounds like Aunt Sis.)

March 20, 1943:

"Dearest Darlin',

They decided on white roses for Ellie's wedding bouquet. *"Gosh honey, I think I'd die if I couldn't come home... We will think of some place to go when I come home, sweet... By the way, dear, you haven't told me what you're going to wear, or aren't I supposed to know?"* He also sent a letter to his folks about their marriage plans.

"Still Your Sweetie Pie

"Love, Emil"

So Ellie and Emil were married on April 3, 1943, at the Old Stone Church in Cleveland, Ohio, with his brother, Bill, and her sister, Dorothy, standing up for them. A reception was held at Ellie's parents' home. They spent their wedding night at the Cleveland Hotel. They also had a one-week honeymoon at the Croydon Hotel in Chicago.

Unfortunately, two weeks after their wedding, Emil and Ellie received some sad news. Ellie's father, William Lohman, passed away from a stroke, and they got an emergency leave to attend the funeral. Ellie remembered that her father always said that he wished he would live long enough to see both of his daughters get married. God granted him his wish. He was seventy years old.

The next letter was postmarked, September 4, 1943, from San Francisco. During the previous four months after the wedding—May, June, July and August—they lived in Boston, Massachusetts, while Emil attended Franklin Institute of

Technology for electrician school. Ellie worked for a dairy company in Cambridge as a comptometer operator. What an exciting time that must have been for them. But it was also filled with apprehension, as they didn't know when or where Emil would be shipped out.

Dad told me that all the married students were allowed to rent and live with their wives, but had to lease their own living quarters. After the first month, orders were given to send the wives home, but Emil and his buddy, Bob, ignored the orders, and every morning, they just fell into line with their classmates going to class and fell out of line after class was done. They were taking a big chance, because if they got caught, they could have suffered a court martial.

Emil on the *Smith Thompson* Ore Ship,
Great Lakes, June 1942-March 1943.

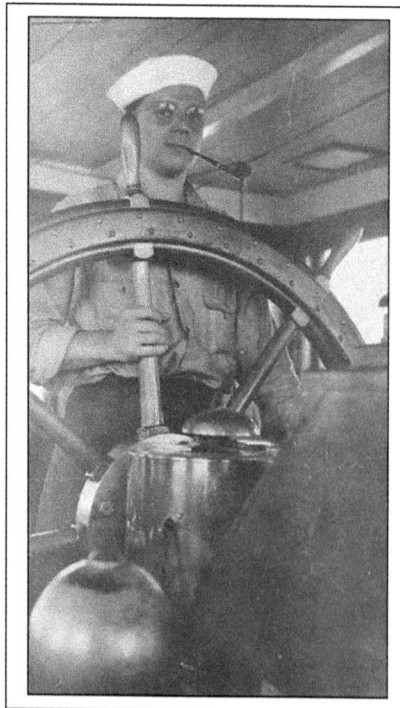

You are cordially invited to
attend "open House" to be held
by Mr. and Mrs. H. Lehman in
honor of the marriage of their
daughter Eldrid June to
Seaman Emil Takacs, at
4328 W. 48 Street, Saturday
April 3, 1943, at 8 o'clock p. m.

P.S. Due to an unexpected
furlough and lack of time
formal announcements could
not be sent.

Ellie and Emil engagement
photo
May 1942

Ellie and Emil Wedding photo
in front yard of W 48th St.

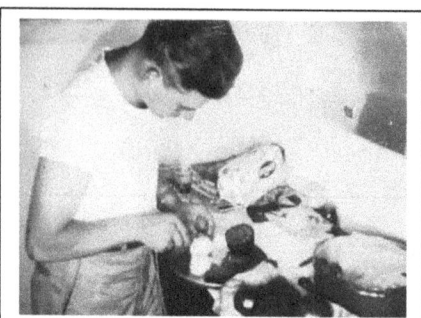

Emil & Buddies, Guard Duty at Seneca,
Hayes Barge Yard 1942

Photos of Emil taken in Chicago, 1943.

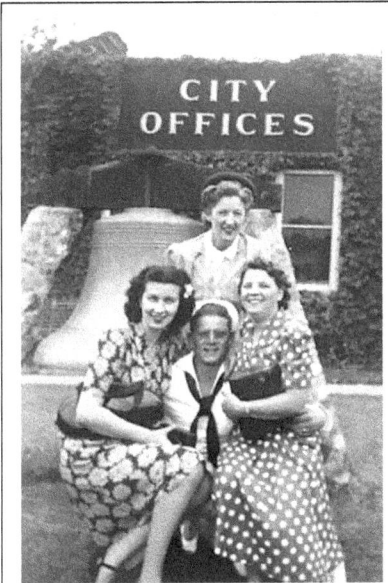

Ellie's visit to Ottawa, IL,
Sept. 1942
Jerry's girlfriend (top), Ellie, Emil,
Rose, Emil's sister-chaperone.

Mr. & Mrs. Takacs

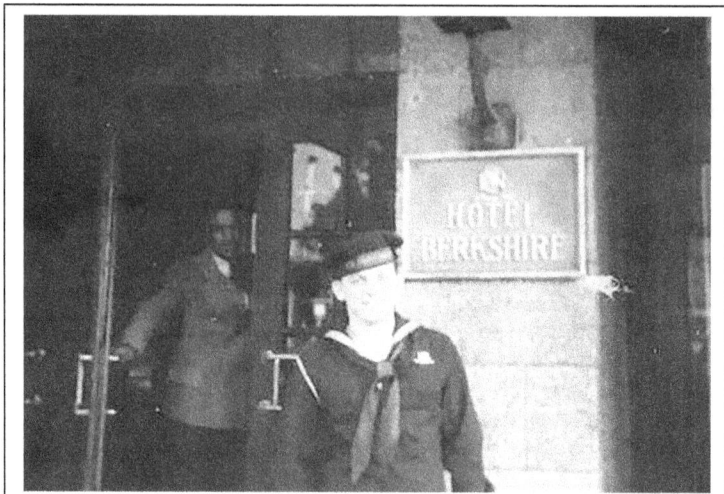

Emil in front of Hotel Berkshire in Chicago, where he stayed from September 1942-March 1943.

Bill Takacs   Emil and Ellie   Dorothy Dew
(Emil's brother)   (Ellie's sister)
Official Wedding photo of
Emil and Ellie Takacs
April 3, 1943, Cleveland, Ohio.

Still Your Sweetie Pie

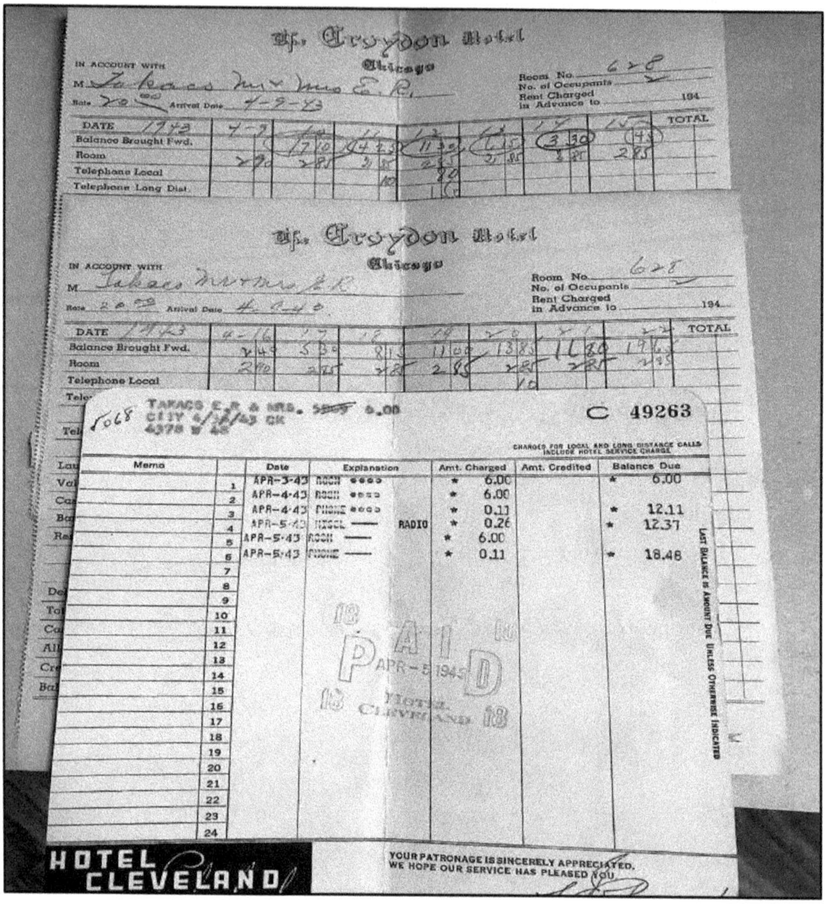

Emil R. Takacs (Tacky)

4378 W. 48th St., Cleveland, Ohio

9th Naval Dist., Chicago, Ill.

SCUTTLEBUTT..... the truth leaks out

Well, fellows, our happy four months have come to an end. During those months the fellows in Group II have come to know each other by certain phrases or certain sayings... By the way, Stevens, did you get that extra piece of meat from the cook today? Now we know why cooks are gray so early in life. After chow we go outside and who do we see taking in the New England sunshine? O.K., Evans, we know the sun doesn't shine in Alaska. And then we run into a certain smell... It's "Tex" Green and his 15-cent cigar.

We move to the corner and here we see the two best "wolves" of our company, Nolan and Shields, giving the girls the glad eye as they walk by. Then muster is called, who is the first one in line... you're "on the ball, Burton". While marching to and from school, we have our soloist, Mr. Takacs, the Grecian serenader... group 12 takes up collection.

In class, who do we bump into, but a guy named McConahey, commonly known as "slide-rule Harry." Hows the slip-stick coming, Harry? We now move down to the gym field and we see a guy making spetacular one-hand catches... who is it? Why, none other than Stefanisk. Then we see "Atlas" coming across the field... nope, we're wrong. It's Max Fuller. What a build! At the other end of the field we see "junior" Bennett, the cigarette man passing out cigarettes to the boys. No wonder... It's the day before payday, and he's the only one who has any left! Coming back from gym, a "Darkie" is seen and the "Oh, Braswell" yell is heard. I'll bet he's from below the Mason-Dixon line. Then we hear another yell... "Hey, fellows, look at the broads!! Who is it? Why it's little Simone, the Revere Flash (he held Paul's horse). Marching back to the Brunswick, we have with us Henry Cheswick, "Tod's gift to the women"... curly in the second row.

Franklin Institute Electrician's School
May 1943, Boston, Mass.
(Emil in second row, 5th from right, squatting down).

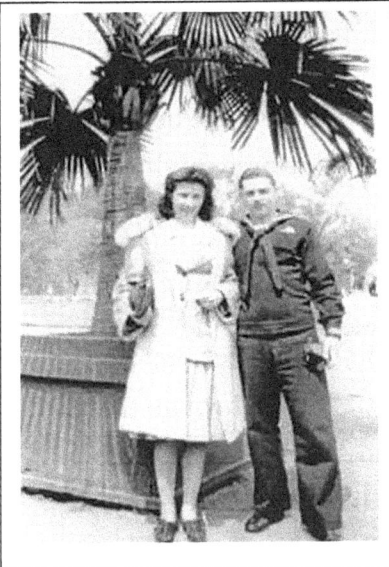

Newlyweds Emil and Ellie
Boston Commons, June 1943

Form No. ▪▪▪   Form Approved. Budget Bureau No. 08-R317

United States of America—Office of Price Administration
APPLICATION FOR WAR RATION BOOK NO. 3

One application must be made for each group of persons who are related by blood, marriage, or adoption and who regularly live at the same address. Persons temporarily away from home (for a period of 60 days or less), such as students, travelers, hospital patients, etc., must be included in the family application. Persons living at the same address BUT NOT RELATED by blood, marriage, or adoption must file SEPARATE applications. If additional applications are needed, you can get them at your post office.

A person may be included in only one application for War Ration Book No. 3.

The following may not apply or be included in any application for War Ration Book No. 3: Persons in the armed services, whether or not eating in organized messes, including Army, Navy, Marines, Coast Guard, and all Women's Auxiliaries; and inmates of institutions of involuntary confinement such as prisons and insane asylums.

Print below full name and complete mailing address of the person to whom books are to be mailed. Books will be delivered by July 21, 1943, to address given below. Books will NOT be forwarded. If you are not reasonably sure of address between June 15 and July 21, 1943, do not submit application. Such applications will be accepted later.

Print in Ink or Type

Name MRS. ELFRID J. TAKHCS

Mailing address 428 MARlborOUGH St.
(Number)   (Street, R. F. D., or General Delivery)

City or post office and State BoSTON , MASSACHUSETTS

№ 37021 M   This application must be mailed

27

Chapter Four

Emil wrote thirteen letters to his new wife between September 4, 1943 and April 25, 1944. The name on the letters now reads: Mrs. E.R. Takacs. How good Emil must have felt to be writing that. Living back home and being separated from Emil must have been very difficult for Ellie. Things were different, now that her loving father had died. But I'm sure she was glad to be helping her mother, Minnie, through this difficult time. She also helped her mother with some foster-child care, as she had done through her teen years.

Emil was shipped to San Francisco, according the postmark of his first letter, where he was eventually reassigned to the Great Lakes Life Boat Station in Michigan City, Indiana.

September 4, 1943:

"Dearest Darlin,

"...haven't gotten any mail for over two months." Emil mentioned that he was anxious to know how Ellie was getting along, and if there were any new additions to the families. He also speaks of all the army nurses and native women that are plentiful, but off-limits to the men *"under penalty of court martial."* (Just what a new wife wants to hear!) Emil *"stood engine-room watches and didn't get sick once this time. I guess I must be getting salty. Ha, Ha!"* he commented.

"Still Your Sweetie Pie,

"Love, Emil"

September 22, 1943—Michigan City, Indiana

"My Dearest Darling,

"Were you worried about me dear?" Emil had moved around so much, he didn't know if he was *"coming or going."* He went from Chicago to St. Joseph, Michigan to Michigan City, Indiana. *"I helped the carpenter sand some floors today, pretty good for an electrician..."* He mentions that this is a small town and now many are here. *"...almost like a morgue."* He explains that she can't come and live with him until he gets settled in his new assignment.

"Give my love to everyone, sweet.

"Still Your Sweetie Pie

"Love, Your Hubby"

September 26, 1943:

"Dearest Darling,

"Golly, it was good to hear from you. I don't know who was more anxious to get a letter, you or I." He explained that he didn't know how long he was going to be here, and for her to be patient until he could send for her. He was keeping busy doing electrical work in the new barracks. It was his first job as an electrician. It was a double feature of cowboy movies. At 12 midnight everything closes. He commented, *"...pretty dull town."*

"Love, Your Hubby"

October 5, 1943:

"Hello Sweetheart,

It sounds like they are really missing each other a lot, as they are trying to make arrangements for a visit or at least a phone call. So hard.

"Listen, dear, please don't let yourself get down by worrying... it doesn't make me feel any too good when you say you don't eat very much... Honey, for my birthday (October 6) all I ask is that you get my ring and watch fixed... I went bowling the other night, but I didn't do so hot. I think I'll have to practice some more." (Emil bowled for a long time after the service. I remember as a child, waiting in the car to pick him up from the bowling alley.)

"Please TAKE CARE OF YOURSELF.

"Love, from your hubby

"P.S. I bought a pair of shoes from the Naval Armory." (Florsheim shoes, $4.50, regular $7.00.)

November 8, 1943—Great Lakes Training Station, Illinios:

"Dearest Darlin',

Emil was here for only a week for anti-aircraft gun training. *"The Coast Guard is a million times better than the Navy,"* he commented.

Apparently they saw each other between October 5 and November 8, because his P.S. says, *"That was a wonderful way to spend our seven-month anniversary, dear. That's one I'll never forget.*

"Still Your Sweetie Pie, Love, Emil"

December 13, 1943:

"Hello Sweetheart,

"There isn't much I can write about today... I have an evening off so I think I'll take in a movie." The temperature was only 10 degrees. *"Gosh, if only we were together, I'm sure neither one of us would freeze.*

"Still Your Sweetie Pie

"Love, Emil"

December 29, 1943:

"Dearest Darlin',

Emil must have been home for Christmas, as he writes: *"Got back safe and sound at 7 a.m. and I was tired."* He was still fixing up the barracks, and he put some wire connections for a heater in a little shanty to stay in while on guard duty so they wouldn't freeze. Their Chief was transferred and everyone was emotional, he mentioned. He also said that he wouldn't be off New Year's Eve, so he couldn't see Ellie.

"Gosh, it was so good to be with you, even if it was for just a short time...

"Still Your Sweetie Pie,

"Love, Emil"

December 30, 1943:

"Hello Sweet,

"...I will call you up between 7-7:30 p.m. New Year's Eve... Well dear, you can still go to that party and have a good time for me, too, honey." Emil was on guard duty from 8 p.m. to

midnight. He comments that the new commanding officer is a *"pretty square fellow."* They also had to patrol the lake in a lifeboat for a missing airplane. *"If everything goes all right I'll be home about the later part of January. So keep your fingers crossed, sweet.*

"Still Your Sweetie Pie

"Love, Emil"

January 16, 1944:

"Hello Darlin,

"...Had 24 hours off... I took a ride to Chicago and saw the Andrews Sisters in person. I hope you're not angry with me for going there, sweet." He also mentions that he went ice skating in the yacht basin. He is also planning his 48-hour leave to come home or have Ellie come up. He was writing this letter from the new rec room they fixed up.

"Gosh, sweet, you're certainly getting a lot of experience with children now. Wait until you'll have to take care of our 10 kids." (Ellie must have been helping her mother with foster children.)

"Still Your Sweetie Pie,

"Love, Emil"

January 31, 1944:

Emil was planning to come home on leave, and he was looking for a place for them to stay together near base. *"Gosh, it's just like spring today and I'm in the mood. Ha, Ha!"* He mentions that he bought his nephew, Andy, another pair of skates, and he suggested that she quit work so they could spend the ten days together.

Emil and Ellie were able to live together from February to April of 1944. There was a postcard with a picture of the Coast Guard Station postmarked March 24, 1944, and addressed to 430 Walker St., Michigan City, Indiana sent from Ludington, Michigan. In the postcard Emil is explaining when he can get a 48 (48-hours leave).

April 11, 1944:

"Hello Honey,

Emil described his adventure returning to base in Ludington City: *"Well, I made it back OK again. I had to stand all the way to Benton Harbor. Then they got another bus and put the 17 of us that were standing, in the reserve one. From Muskegon I got a ten-mile ride, and from there the driver of the first bus had his own car and gave me a ride to Ludington's city limits. From there I walked to the station. It took me about a half an hour. I was in bed by 3:30."* (Such an ordeal!)

Apparently Ellie was going back to Cleveland for a visit. He also mentioned that he played a game of hearts and won 75 cents.

April 20, 1944:

"Hello Dearest,

"Well how did it feel to go for a train ride again and see

the folks? Just so you're not too tired and worn out by this weekend."

His writing got sloppy at this point, and he explained that the *"boys are horsing around... what a bunch of screwballs."* While it felt good to take a boat out once in a while, he mentioned he likes *"the good old earth the better of the two."*

"See you sometime this weekend.

"Still Your Sweetie Pie,

"Love, Emil"

April 25, 1944:

"Hello Honey,

(Returning from the weekend.) *"About 20 minutes after we left you, I started everybody singing, and we kept it up for about three hours. It passed the time, anyway. I didn't get a seat until we reached South Haven, and that sure felt good."* He got to Muskegon at 12:30 a.m., and hitched a ride to base and got back there at 2 a.m.

They cleaned some motors, and he complained that all they were learning was how to get dirty. *"...it seems like such a waste of time over here...*

"Still Your Sweetie Pie,

"Love, Emil"

Those last words were prophetic, because Emil was soon to be shipped overseas for eighteen months, during the remainder of the war.

Chapter Five

April 30, 1944:

Ellie received a postcard from Emil from Barstow, California, and it was addressed to her childhood home in Cleveland, Ohio. In those five, short days, Emil received orders to ship out, and Ellie had to pack quickly and head home, not knowing when or if they would see each other again. How difficult that must have been. They had been married one year and 27 days.

First Letter from Alameda, CA, dated May 2, 1944:

"Hello Sweetheart,

Emil's group traveled by train to California. They were six hours late getting into Barstow and had a ten-hour layover before reaching the base in Alameda, which is about five miles from Oakland.

"Well, this is California, and so far the weather has been perfect. In the evening it gets nice and cool, and in the daytime you bask under the California sunshine, which is really wonderful." He wrote this letter while lying on the grass on the reservation, *"...watching the fellows play baseball."*

Emil met up with a buddy he met at the University of Chicago who was also writing to his wife. He described him as, *"...a small fellow. It was a relief to have him keep me company."* (I imagine a familiar face was very comforting.)

Emil mentioned that Ellie wouldn't be able to come out there, and he lamented, *"I miss you SO much."*

"Still Your Sweetie Pie,

"Love, Emil"

(Editor's note: Most of the letters were neatly opened at the end, but this one was ripped open. I can imagine Ellie coming home at the end of her work day and anxiously tearing open the treasured letter, especially since he was so far away now.)

May 4, 1944:

"Hi Dearest,

Emil learned that he had to report to another barracks tomorrow for his ship duty assignment. Once again he was lying out on the grass and said how well they were being treated. *"No watches, just lay around and be present for roll call three times a day."* They even brought in entertainment from Los Angeles. He mentioned taking a liberty to see San Francisco and was disappointed. *"It's nothing but a crowded, filthy city."* Emil told Ellie not to worry too much.

"SYSP Love, Emil"

May 15, 1944:

The letters were sent airmail and cost $.08 cents. (Imagine that!)

"Hello Sweetheart,

Emil was still awaiting orders and all he was doing was cleaning the quarters and sweeping the streets. He joked,

"Maybe I can get a job with the city after the war is over."

He went on to explain that they were interviewing electricians for *"a special mission of which I'm not allowed to disclose."* He said he didn't think he'd be going, because there were others with more experience.

The mail service was terrible out there, and he complained he only received two letters from Ellie, and that was because he looked through the discarded mail. (How many misunderstandings and anxious moments must have been caused by this delay?)

He watched two movies, "Shine on Harvest Moon" and "Buffalo Bill." *"The first was the better of the two,"* he said.

Ellie was working at Marshall's, and Emil cautioned her not to work too much overtime and not to worry too much about him.

"SYSP Love, Emil"

May 25, 1944 (from Wilmington, CA, a Receiving Station) written on USO paper:

"Hello Dearest,

Emil was now in Long Beach, CA, where he was assigned to one of the Army Transport ships. (These ships were only 99 ½ feet long with a 13-man crew. They landed in New Guinea after two months of travel, and only 11 out of 33 ships made it to their destination. [Glad he was on one of the ships that made it!])

"We don't know as yet when our ship will pull out and am sorry to say that I can't tell you much about our ship and duties, as we are given strict orders not to do so." He can't send for her

(in Long Beach) he explains, because he didn't know how long he would be there—weeks or months. He would be the only electrician aboard the ship and would be very busy, he was told. He asked Ellie to extend anniversary greetings to his sister Tillie and her husband, Andy.

"SYSP Love, Emil"

May 29, 1944:

"Dearest Darlin',

Ellie must have started a beauty course, because Emil inquired about it. He explained that he was keeping busy repairing electrical equipment. He mentioned that he might visit Hollywood on the next liberty. The crew was getting familiar with the ship before going out to sea, and he liked the crew and officers. He was anxiously awaiting news from home about the *"...new addition in the Gedeon family,"* (Carl Jr.). *"Gee honey, each line I write I want to tell you how VERY MUCH I MISS YOU, but I can't express it well enough."*

"SYSP, Love Emil

June 3, 1944:

"Dearest Darlin,

Emil hadn't received a letter from Ellie while at the Receiving Station, and he finally received letter #7. (He suggested she number her letters so he could keep track of them.) It took three days for a letter to arrive from Ohio to CA via airmail. He finally found out that his sister, Rose, had given birth to Carl Jr. *"Why, I was on pins and needles wondering how sis was getting along. I'm certainly glad it was a boy, though.*

(They had two girls, Rosemarie and Doris.) *I can just imagine how proud Carl* (brother-in-law) *feels."*

Emil said that he and Ellie would get quite a workout when he got home, trying to catch up with children to their three sisters, Dorothy, Rose and Tillie. (Cute.)

Emil explained that by now he was quite confident that he could repair any electrical problem on the ship.

Many of his letters were signed off with, *"Give my love to all, Darlin', and take EXTRA GOOD CARE OF YOURSELF.*

"SYSP Love, Emil

June 7, 1944:

"Hello Sweetheart? No, I'll say my darling wife this time,"

Emil went to see Hollywood and wasn't very impressed. *"I saw Grauman's Chinese Theatre, the Hollywood Bowl and the Hollywood Canteen, which is nothing but a joint, and a few of the motion picture studios."*

The crew painted the anchor chain and were covered with *"red and black spots all over our bodies from the waist to the tip of our heads."* Emil asked about Ellie's beauty school and said he had received another picture of her.

"SYSP Love, Emil

"PPSS: Honey, would you please send me the recipe for chicken paprikash!"

June 15, 1944: (Included a cocktail napkin from Long Beach.)

"Hello Sweetheart,

They were preparing for their cruise as the crew all chipped in and bought a Victrola and they stocked up on tobacco, too. Emil noted that he spent about $25 to get ready for the cruise, which included some clothes, too. He was having a hard time finding a June 19th birthday gift for Ellie. *"Dearest, I've looked all over this town for a certain thing I wanted to give you on your birthday, but all of them were too cheap looking, so until I'm able to find a good one, I hope this little sum of money will express some of my feeling for your birthday, sweetheart.*

>   *"SYSP Love, Emil*

>   *"PPSS: Hold the mail for a while, dear."* (Must have been expecting to be shipped out.)

June 29, 1944: (Ellie's 25th birthday.)

>   *"Dearest Darlin',*

>   *"Well honey, this will be the last letter from me for a while... so don't get worried if you don't hear from me for a while."* The ship was heading out, and he didn't know when they'd be able to get mail through. Emil explained that he had hitched a ride into town and to his surprise ran into a neighbor that used to live across the street from him. (Imagine the comfort of seeing someone from home while so far away.)

He expressed his concern about sending or receiving letters for a while. *"Gosh, am I going to miss those letters, honey, that's about the only way I can keep from getting lonesome, dear.*

>   *"SYSP Love, Emil"*

IT TOOK ONE MONTH FOR THE NEXT LETTER.

July 14, 1944:

(Postmarked San Francisco—noticed that the letters now have a NAVAL CENSOR stamp on the envelope, indicating that they have been checked for any war information.)

"My Darlin' Wife,

"We have arrived at our first hopping off place, you might well guess where that is. Boy this time I really can't tell you a damn thing, because the mail is censored, and I do mean censored..."

Emil wrote that he was feeling fine, except for seasickness the first few days, and *"...getting a beautiful tan."* He was doing electrical work and doing *"wheel watches,"* in case of an attack. He mentioned that he hadn't shaved for eight days, and some of the other fellows now had mustaches like he did. (He'd acquired his earlier, growing it on a bet. And he wore that mustache all of his life.) He also bragged that he did his own laundry—the whites and the blues.

"SYSP Love, Emil"

THREE WEEKS LATER

August 4, 1944:

"Dearest Darlin',

Emil was now able to tell Ellie that their first stop was Honolulu because they were at their next port. They could not send anything home with the name on, until they got to the next port. He described Honolulu as *"...just a crowded sailor town with nothing to do but walk."* He said Waikiki was beautiful. They heard a Hawaiian Royal Band which was good. He requested more snapshots from home. *"They would certainly help a lot,"* he commented.

"SYSP Love, Emil

"PPSS: I love you and miss you terribly honey."

ONE MONTH LATER

Postmarked September 9 (written on August 31) **1944:**

"My Dearest Darlin',

He wrote that he still hadn't received any letters from her. *"I do hope some will come soon."* Now they were in New Guinea. He said that he sent his sister Tillie a shell necklace as a birthday gift for his niece Barbie. He bought it with Australian money, which was the only currency on the island. They got to hear broadcasts on the radio dedicated to the armed forces and listened to the baseball scores. *"Boy, the Indians are taking a beating this year."*

He asked about all of the infants in the *"three happy households."* (That was a reference to his sister Rose and her baby, Carl Jr., and his sister Tillie and Barbie and Andy Jr., and Ellie's sister Dorothy and her babies, Nancy and Gary.)

"SYSP Love, Emil"

September 15, (Written August 6) **1944:**

"My Dearest Darlin,

Finally, Emil wrote that he received letters for the first time since he'd left the states. He got numbers 2-7. He proceeded to answer Ellie's questions and commented on her letters. Mentioned Carl Gedeon getting hurt on vacation, and Orville Dew (Dorothy's husband) passing his sergeant's police exam.

"Yes, we have fairly good food, but my weight has stayed around the 155# mark." He spoke of Rosemarie's kidney illness and of the possibility of them taking a second honeymoon. They had been seeing some good family movies in New Guinea, and they were hoping that Bob Hope would be one of the stage show guests. Emil requested a Kaywoodie pipe for his birthday, October 6.

"SYSP Love, Emil—your seasick (sailor) husband"

September 27 (Written September 19) **1944:**

"My Dearest Darlin',

Emil was going to number his letters now. This was #1. He was glad to hear Ellie finally received the pillowcase and tablecloth he sent from Hawaii.

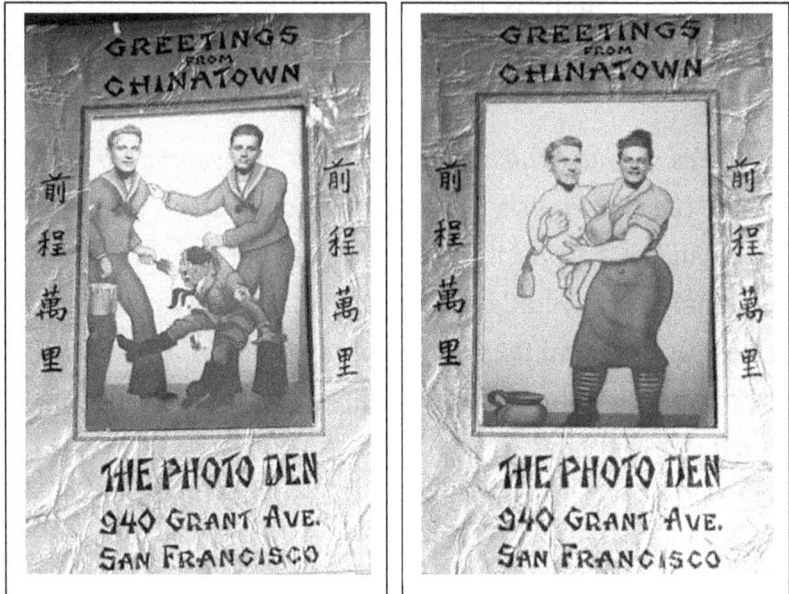

Emil and a Buddy, May 1944.

October 10, 1944:

Emil had received a bunch of letters and pictures from Ellie all at once. (This was very common during the war.) He commented on the condition of the photos and how much it meant to receive them. *"Gosh, Andy Jr. is quite grown since I last saw him."* (Emil's nephew.) *"Rose really looks wonderful after having her latest addition."* (Carl Gedeon, Emil's nephew).

Duties in New Guinea included making short trips carrying cargo in an F-7 boat.

Both Emil and Ellie had seen the movie, "Up in Arms," with Danny Kay. *"He really is a screwball. I never laughed so hard in a long time,"* Emil commented. He also requested that Ellie send him a box of cigars once in a while.

"I've still got my mustache..." Emil told her. He also asked her to send film size 610, as one of the men had a camera that size. Then he could send her a snapshot of himself. Ellie really enjoyed going to the cottage at Chippewa Lake with Emil's family. Emil said he was sending home a gift—a P-38 ashtray made from bullet shells by the servicemen. (That was given to Emil's grandson, Mark Johnston.)

This particular letter was three pages long, front and back. Ellie requested that he write long letters.

October 21, 1944:

"My Dearest Darlin',

"I've just been transferred off the F-7 for chronic seasickness, ain't I a hell of a sailor... hope you won't be too ashamed of me for being transferred for that..." Emil also wrote that Ellie was *"...putting in too much extra work,"* and cautioned her to take care of herself.

October 26, 1944:

"My Dearest Darlin',   '

Still waiting for new orders. Emil confessed what could have been a tragedy—he lost his wedding ring. Fortunately, after it was missing a week, someone found it in the rag barrel! Then Emil remembered filling the barrel with rags on the day the ring had disappeared. One can only imagine how relieved Emil was. *"...will watch it more closely now, dear,"* Emil promised.

Emil also mentioned that he hadn't gotten paid for seven weeks, so Ellie's Christmas money order might be delayed.

(He got paid $21 a month for the first three months, and then he got a pay raise with each promotion. He was up to $50 a month. He started as a 2nd class seaman, then 1st class seaman, Petty officer 3rd class, Petty officer 2nd class. That was as high as he could go when he was head electrician on the Murzim.)

"I love you and miss you more than you'll ever know. I may not show it in my letters, but I mean it with all my heart, dear.

"Still Your Sweetie Pie,

"Love, Emil"

October 27, 1944:

Still waiting for new orders......

"My Dearest Darlin',

Emil promised to try to write more often. He said their captain complimented his unit on the cleanliness of their barracks. He also sent Ellie the papers for crossing the Equator and the 180th Meridian and asked her to frame them. Also, apparently, he survived some kind of initiation and didn't get his head shaved. (Wonder what that was all about!)

[*Note: The ceremony observes a mariner's transformation from slimy Pollywog, a seaman who hasn't crossed the equator, to a trusty Shellback, also called a 'Son of Neptune'. It was a way for sailors to be tested for their seaworthiness.]

He sent home some extra clothes, because he just needed "dungarees" (jeans) and a few uniforms. *"...don't get frightened when you receive them,"* he wrote. Otherwise he wasn't doing much. (The waiting must have been nerve-wracking and boring.)

"SYSP Love, Emil"

October 30, 1944:

Still waiting.....

"My Dearest Darlin',

Emil saw a lousy movie called "Coastal Command," an English picture. He answered brother Bill and niece Rosemarie's letters and asked Ellie how her beauty course was coming. *"How about a finger wave, honey? Ha! Ha!"* (Emil had naturally wavy hair.) *"As soon as I finish this letter I'm going to church. I've been going regularly lately. Aren't I good, dear?*

"SYSP Love, Emil"

November 4, 1944:

Still waiting.....

"Dearest Sweetheart,

Emil sent Ellie $75 for her to use to buy herself a Christmas present. *"I hope by next Xmas I'll be home and I might be able to get you more, honey. I know I can't give you what a wonderful wife like you deserves, sweet..."*

He mentioned he was being transferred to another ship.

"SYSP Love, Emil"

November 8, 1944:

"Dearest Darlin',

They had some boxing matches in the ring on base. *"...some of the boys really slugged it out... Honey, that was a very nice letter you wrote, the one you called mushy, and I was not bored with it Dear. Sweet, that's the only thing I wait for now, is your letters. Just keep writing as many and as often as you can."*

Emil was concerned that Ellie was working overtime so much. (I'm sure she did it to make the time go faster.) He also wondered when she would send a package. *"...But I have everything I need here, that is except you, dear."*

"SYSP Love, Emil"

November 22, 1944:

Still waiting......

"My Dearest Darlin',

"It seems every place we go, the ship is elsewhere. Maybe by the time the war is over we'll catch up with it. I sure would like to get settled again and stop this chasing around." (Apparently, the small boat was trying to catch up with the Murzim.) He mentioned that he hadn't received any of the packages that Ellie had sent. *"I'm now in the* (censored—cut out [Manus Islands]) *at the receiving station waiting further orders."* He described that these were the best barracks in the South Pacific area and they were allowed to take showers anytime and could also buy a full box of cigars!

Emil inquired about things at home and hoped everything was going normally.

"SYSP Love, Emil"

December 4, 1944:

Still waiting......

"Dearest Darlin',

"How is my honey doing today? Have you all your Xmas shopping done?" Emil inquired. He also asked Ellie to have the

ashtray engraved with the name of the island or base (that name was censored and cut out of the letter).

Emil complained he still hadn't received all of the letters Ellie had sent and he cautioned her again about working long hours. He also complained about too much rain and how it took so long for their clothes to dry.

"SYSP Love, Emil"

December 17, 1944:

Still waiting......

"Dearest Darlin',

FINALLY Emil received two letters from Ellie and one from sister Rose and niece Rosemarie. He hadn't gotten any mail for two months. (How awful that must have been.)

"Thanks for the pictures, dear. It's the best Xmas present you can give me now, and honey you look swell... is Carl Jr. really cute as you've written me?"

Emil mentioned that he saw a pretty good movie, "San Diego I Love You," with Jim Hall and Louise AlBritton and a "Mighty Mouse Cartoon." He also said that sister Rose sent him a fruit cake, but he didn't think he would ever get it.

"PPSS: Gosh, dear, I forgot to mention that midnight last night my enlistment was up, but I won't be able to change my papers until I get aboard the Murzim. I can't believe I've spent three years in the service already, although it has seemed like a lifetime."

"SYSP Love, Emil"

December 22, 1944: (Photo of Ellie enclosed)

"My Dearest Darlin',

Still waiting........

"Well, only three more days till Xmas. Oh happy day." (A little sarcasm there—I can only imagine how much harder it was to keep their spirits up with the holidays approaching.)

Emil spoke of only having to work a single shift instead of a double, and that he wrote sister Rose and brother-in-law Carl a letter. *"If I had more news to give out I'd write more, but it's pretty hard writing about nothing, with the exception of telling how very, very much I love and miss you, sweet.*

"PPSS: Please forgive this short letter, dear. I know you understand." (I could sense the depression Emil felt.)

"SYSP Love, Emil"

December 26, 1944:

"My Darlin' Wife,

"I certainly hope you've had a better Xmas then we did on this Island. We did have a good meal, although we had to work the night shift missing the special Xmas night state show. It wouldn't have been so bad working if we would have done something worthwhile. All we did was move canned goods from one end of the warehouse to the other..." Emil griped. He also complained that they couldn't go to communion if you're on a working party.

Emil related a joke he found in the Island newspaper: *"Modern girls wear sweaters and their mothers do the sweating."* (Such innocence during such a turbulent time.)

"SYSP Love, Emil"

Ellie, Rose, Doris

Ellie and Dorie

1944

It was a sad Christmas in 1944 with Emil overseas.
Fortunately it was their only Christmas apart.

December 30, 1944:

"Dearest Darlin,

Still waiting..........

"Well, honey, in a couple of more days we'll be having a New Year, and we have yet to spend a New Year's together. Just think, dear, it won't be long and we'll be able to spend all the

rest of the holidays together forever. Honey, that's about all I think of is when I'll be with you always," Emil promised.

The enlisted men were "peeved" because on Xmas the officers got drunk and they couldn't get one glass of beer. "It's things like that that turn the boys against the officers." He saw the "Miracle of Morgan's Creek," a movie he always wanted to see. "That was about one of the funniest pictures I've seen for a while," Emil said. He mentioned he smoked a Camel cigarette and that he hoped he hadn't griped too much in this letter.

"SYSP Love, Emil"

New Year January 1, 1945:

"My Darlin' Wife,

Still waiting.........

"Well dear, another exciting year has passed. Oh Happy Day!"

The men saw the New Year in with a little stage show, a few boxing and wrestling matches, and a movie. "About 11:30 we had some sandwiches and coffee, and then at mid-night I gave some of the boys cigars, and that's how we brought the New Year in. Exciting, wasn't it?"

*Ellie wrote something special on an envelope: "But honey, all this time I didn't stop thinking one min-ute about you. Darling, no matter where I am or what I'm do-ing, somehow or other you're always before me reminding me of a wonderful day when we'll be together always." (That's our romantic mom.)

The guys were surprised to get their second day off in six weeks, also.

"SYSP Love, Emil"

January 9, 1945:

"Hello Sweetheart,

Still waiting.......

Another day off for Emil—He listened to Groucho Marx and Frank Morgan on the radio. *"It was a darn good program. They recited a poem: 'Roses are red, violets are blue. I know Violet's are blue because I saw them hanging on the line yester-day.' Ha-Ha! The whole program was full of wisecracks,"* Emil said.

They had peachès for breakfast and *"for once they weren't too bad."* They usually had them once a week. They built a little recreation center for the guys to write letters, read magazines, look at maps and play ping pong.

"Honey, I hope you're getting along well. How is your money holding out? Dear, don't hesitate to ask for any money, because I'll feel terrible if you needed something and couldn't get it. As long as I can do it, I want my wife to have everything that I can possibly give her."

"SYSP Love, Emil"

Chapter Six

The next 26 letters from January 26, 1945 through August 19, 1945 were written while Emil was on the ammunition ship, *The USS Murzim* in the South Pacific during WWII. Ellie didn't know it was an ammunition ship, for obvious reasons. Now the letters were being censored. There is a censor stamp on the envelope and staple holes on the end of the envelope where the censors have opened them and stapled them closed. Also some letters have words cut out, which was the consequence when Emil inadvertently let a destination be disclosed.

Postmarked January 26, 1945: (Written January 23; First letter from the Murzim.)

"My Dearest Darlin',

The crew left on short notice from the shore station which was in San Pedro, CA. When he got aboard he received 35 letters, dated from November 2 to January 5. The December letters were missing. He received those at a later date. Emil sent Ellie papers, an ash tray and a bracelet. He was worried about his sea bag getting home. He mentioned that he was glad to hear she went out with her girlfriends and told her what a beautiful figure she had in the picture she sent. He also talked about his niece, Doris, and how the guys wanted to date her when she got older, because her photo was so beautiful. He was hoping he could get home for Christmas. AND HE DID! But they didn't know that then.

Emil described the ship: *"It's pretty large, but doesn't go as fast as I thought it would. The crew seems pretty nice, and we have cool quarters. Our lockers are about two feet square all around... plenty of room... chow isn't bad... nice electrician shop to work in."* He couldn't tell her anymore, because the censor might cut it out. *"Darn them, anyway,"* he complained.

Ellie was taking a beauty school course at this time, and Emil encouraged her, but he was always worried about her working too hard. Uncle Carl, sister Rose's husband, was using Emil's bowling ball. Emil thought that was good, because Carl was like a father to him. He kidded that he would let his mustache grow into handlebars.

"Still Your Sweetie Pie"

Postmarked January 26, 1945: (Written January 24; Second letter from the Murzim.)

"Dearest Darlin',

Emil received a letter from Ellie and niece Rosemarie. He thought Rosemarie should become a humorist. Ellie must have spent Thanksgiving with Emil's mother and family, because he thanked her for doing that. He was enjoying a cigar while writing this letter. Ellie sent him some clippings of a snowstorm, also. She said she had to wear flannel pajamas, and he kidded, *"Well, you certainly won't need them when I get home, dear. Ha! Ha!"*

He asked her to have the ashtray he sent her from New Guinea engraved with the year 1944. He spoke of Rosemarie's six-foot boyfriend that Carl's mother takes care of. *"The picture you sent holding Carl Jr. was very cute, and the bottom half of you, well that was good too! Ha! Ha!"*

"Still Your Sweetie Pie

"PSS: Goodnight 'Funny Face'"

February 6, 1945: (Third letter from the Murzim.)

"Dearest Darlin',

"Just think, dear, this morning for the first time in about five months I had real sunny-side up eggs." He had arrived at another port. He was excited about going onshore for liberty. He said Ellie wouldn't be getting mail regularly, because they couldn't send mail until they *"hit port."* He sent her Jap invasion money. There were two pups and a mother dog on board ship. "Sad Sack " and "General Quarters" were their names.

"Still Your Sweetie Pie"

February 9, 1945: (Fourth letter from the Murzim.)

"Dearest Darlin',

He finally received her December 26th letter in which she described her Christmas. *"Dearest, I know how hard it is our being separated, but I know we can stick it out a little longer. Just keep in thought, sweet, the day that I will be home to stay..."* He mentioned that he saw movies, "Adventures of Mark Twain", "The Angels Sing" and "Two Girls and a Sailor."

Postmarked February 20, 1945: (Written February 15; Fifth letter from the Murzim.)

"Dearest Darlin'

Just Have The Band Play Stardust

If you want to make me sentimental
I only know one way.
Just have the band play "Stardust"
And Darling, I'll obey.
#

You don't have to treat me kind and gentle
When skies above are gray,
Just sing the words to "Stardust"
And the clouds will sail away.
#

There's something 'bout that dream song
That sets my heart aglow.
Let's keep it for our theme song
Through the years that come and go.
#

And if fate should ever come between us
To leave a memory
I'll have the band play "Stardust"
To bring you back to me.

Emil asked forgiveness for not remembering Valentine's Day sooner. He sent the poem, "Just have the Band Play Stardust," as her Valentine gift. He saw the movie, "When Irish Eyes are Smilin'." He got paid twice a month. And he had taken out a loan and was paying it back, so his pay was only $9.00.

"Still Your Sweetie Pie"

Postmarked March 5, 1945: (Written March 2; Sixth letter from the Murzim.)

"Dearest Darlin',

Emil apologized for not writing sooner. He was busy with lighting equipment. His mail was coming in order now. He had received Ellie's February 20th letter and again express-ed concern about her working so hard. It's Saturday, and he finished his washing, but he had nowhere to relax on the ship. Some guy was bothering him while he was trying to write this letter.

"Still Your Sweetie Pie"

March 5, 1945: (Seventh letter from the Murzim.)

"Dearest Darlin,"

Emil was worried about Ellie's headaches... *"Wish that I could express the love that I have for you on paper, but until I'll be able to see you again, you'll just have to dream of it, dear."* He got $6.00 this payday and mentioned the debt was paid off. The lost mail bags were found—he got a box of cigars from his sister Tillie—half were moldy, but he shared the rest with the guys. A lot of packages came for the guys, but were beyond recognition and had to be thrown away. SO SAD.

"Still Your Sweetie Pie"

March 8, 1945: (Eighth letter from the Murzim.)

"Dearest Darlin',

Emil received Ellie's letters today—one dated January 16, and one February 26. He sent Ellie a one-pound note of Australian money. It was worth a little over three dollars of US money, so she kept it for a souvenir. Emil was going to see "Tender Comrades" movie. He hoped it was good, because the last ones were lousy, he complained. He spent time rearranging electrical equipment in the hot weather and was sweating. *"As I mentioned before dear, if you don't receive any mail from me for a while, be patient, honey, as we're probably out at* (Censor cutout) *somewhere.*

"Still Your Sweetie Pie"

Postmarked March 25, 1945: (Written March 22; Ninth letter from the Murzim.)

"My Dearest Darlin',

"Well, dear, I haven't any gifts or even an anniversary card to send to you on our forthcoming wedding Anniversary (April 3, 1943). The only thing that I can say or send to you will be in words, and darling believe me with all my heart when I say I've never known happiness to be so great as the days of them we've had together, dear. I'm looking forward to the day when we'll be able to continue them for always." (AND THEY DID FOR 55 YEARS!)

One of the crew members from a former ship who was the motor mechanic joined Emil on this ship. He was surprise- ed to see him. Most of the Murzim crew were almost done with their 18 months at sea. Emil had been there nine months and had nine more to go, unless the war ended first. (He spent seven months on the ship.) He mentioned he had good meals of chicken, turkey and steaks. *"Not bad, huh?"*

"Still Your Sweetie Pie"

Postmarked March 30, 1945: (Written March 27; Tenth letter from the Murzim.)

"My Dearest Darlin',

"The news from Europe sounds pretty good doesn't it. All we can hope for now is to get it over with quick, so that we may all return to a normal life again." Emil was going to write a letter to Ellie's sister Dorothy and husband Orville. He asked about their children, Gary and Nancy. He had been busy fixing fans aboard ship. He said they all seemed to go bad at once.

"Still Your Sweetie Pie"

April 26, 1945: (Eleventh letter from the Murzim.)

"My Dearest Darlin',

Ellie had sent some pictures from Easter, and he said he liked them. He was busy doing interior decorating in the electrician shop on board ship. They painted it powder blue-gray. The bottom part was trimmed in dark gray. Emil also commented on Marshall's department store closing down, and he mentioned President Roosevelt's death. Emil still got seasick, but he stuck it out, now. He was going to take a "bucket bath." These were the type of baths they took on the "F Boats." Because of limited space, each man was issued one bucket of water to bathe, drink and brush teeth with each day. When they got on the Murzim, they took salt-water showers, which Emil said made his hair gummy. The guys still called them "bucket baths."

* (Note: Their clothing had to be rolled up when put in the sea bag to keep it from wrinkling. They were trained how to do that in boot camp. Emil had a bottle of bleach in his bag and it broke and ruined 75% of his clothes, so he was issued new ones.)

Postmarked May 21, 1945: (Written May 18; Twelfth letter from the Murzim.)

"Dearest Darlin',

Emil writes that he hadn't received any mail for three weeks. In the letter they were planning the type of home they wanted after he returned. He also thanked Ellie for some newspaper clippings. And he spoke of nieces Rosemarie and Doris, his sister Rose and Carl's daughters. He mentioned planning to see some crew members after the war when they visited Cleveland. Emil complimented Ellie on her "hair setting" skill learned in beauty school.

"PSS: I love you honey and miss you very much.

"Still Your Sweetie Pie"

Postmarked June 6, 1945: (Written June 1; Thirteenth letter from the Murzim.)

"Dearest Darlin',

"...On the go somewhere in (censored)...

Finally in civilization after 12 months at sea, Emil got a promotion to Second Class. The weather here was like Frisco, and they had to wear their dress blues and pea coats. It was a nice relief from the hot weather in the tropics, he said. Everyone was cleaning and pressing their dress blues, because now that they were in civilization they could go ashore. He would be able to send more mail now, and he hoped they would be here for a *"long spell."* Emil learned to play cribbage here. It was a card game that he played all of his life. It uses a deck of cards and a board with holes and pegs to count the score. (He

61

taught his daughters the game, and they enjoyed it and still have his cribbage board.)

"Still Your Sweetie Pie"

Postmarked June 6, 1945: (Written June 3; Fourteenth letter from the Murzim.)

"My Dearest Darlin',

"In my last letter dated June 1, the censors probably had a field day, as I've just found out that our position at present cannot be revealed... I'm in civilization and it sure feels wonderful. Just think, dear, I had fresh milk, tomatoes, cucumbers, and lemons for the first time in about twelve months." Emil had his first night ashore and had a cherry malted milkshake, a T-bone steak dinner, and lettuce and tomato salad. *"It feels good to see civilization again, but... there's nothing like you and the states,"* Emil confessed. He mentioned that his monthly pay was $145.00 and Ellie's allotment checks would be $75.00. He commented that he was going to eat turkey today, since it was Sunday.

"Still Your Sweetie Pie"

Postmarked June 9, 1945: (Written June 7; Fifteenth letter from the Murzim.)

"Hello My Dearest Darlin',

"Just as I started writing this letter, one of the boys remembered that today was his anniversary, and now we're all trying to help him figure out a way so that his wife won't find out about his forgetfulness, but it looks like he'll just have to admit the truth to her. Boy, is he in a mess." Emil mentioned

that he was sending Ellie her birthday present and hoped it would get there in time for June 19.

A lot about food in this letter: the meal on the ship was fresh lettuce and tomato salad, fresh mashed potatoes and gravy, fresh milk and bread, roast mutton and one pint of ice cream for each crew member. *"Boy, were we full,"* Emil admitted. Then he had a chicken dinner at one of the few classy restaurants and apple-banana pie with ice cream. *"That should put some weight on me. Ha! Ha!"* he hoped. He wanted to tell her where they were , but said they weren't allowed to say one word about their location. (It was Australia.)

"Still Your Sweetie Pie"

Postmarked June 11, 1945: (Written June 9; Sixteenth letter from the Murzim.)

"My Dearest Darlin',

They were experiencing the rainy season (in Australia). Emil asked Ellie if she figured out where they were yet. He was still worried about her birthday gift and card, since they didn't have much of a selection. *"...this place is terrible for buying gifts."* He received more snapshots of Ellie and said how proud he was to show them off to the boys on board. They were cleaning up the ship, preparing to sail again. *"Oh happy day. Bah!"* Emil complained. He made some comments about family members: niece Doris, Ellie's mother, Minnie, and his brother-in-law Andy, married to his sister, Tillie. And again Emil was worried about Ellie's health, suggesting she stay home from work when she's sick. She mentioned she was going to the family's cottage at Chippewa Lake (near Medina,

Ohio) for a vacation. (The cottage was purchased in 1937 by the Lukcso and Gedeon families and then sold to Andy Lukcso's sister in 1941.) Emil's family loved Ellie and were always happy when she came to the cottage.

"Still Your Sweetie Pie"

Postmarked June 17, 1945: (Written June 13; Seventeenth letter from the Murzim.)

"Dearest Darlin',

Emil had just received a letter from Ellie dated May 31. He complained about the poor mail service. He commented on his brother-in-law, Carl, with whom the family lived. *"...Carl really is very understanding and thoughtful. I know myself I'll never be able to repay him for what he's done for me all these years..."* (When Emil was seven, his father bought him a new pair of shoes which were too small, and then he left the family. That was the last time Emil ever saw him. When Emil was 11, he and his mother and sister Tillie went to live with his married sister Rose and her husband Carl. Carl was like a father to Emil.)

Emil mentioned he was enjoying listening to Straus's Waltzes on the radio. *"I don't think there's any music better than his..."* The men were getting lots of milk and ice cream now and gaining back weight they had lost at sea. *"I saw the news reals last night of the victory in Europe. Boy, they sure looked to be having a big celebration, but that isn't near as good as the one we're going to have when this side is beaten, Huh, Sweet!"*

"Still Your Sweetie Pie"

Postmarked June 18, 1945: (Written June 15; Eighteenth letter from the Murzim.)

"My Dearest Darlin',

"How's my honey today? Feeling good, I hope." Emil received a letter from his niece, Rosemarie, telling about all of her boyfriends. He remarks to Ellie, *"Even though we're in civilization, it certainly isn't like home. What I wouldn't give just to be with you for a few days.. Well, I can dream, can't I?"* He also wrote about mail packages coming in for the boys today and said he was sending Ellie another little souvenir between two blocks of wood that she would have to pry apart. Said she would get it in a couple of weeks. Emil mentioned that he was on duty tonight and had to do some repairs. Meatloaf, mashed potatoes and gravy, lettuce and cucumber salad, radishes, sliced peaches and pears and milk were on the menu that night. *"Darn it, no ice cream,"* he complained.

"Still Your Sweetie Pie"

Postmarked June 21, 1945: (Written June 18; Nineteenth letter from the Murzim.)

"My Dearest Darlin',

"Hello honey, forgive me for not writing for a couple of days. I've been feeling rough, but I'm O.K. now." One of the guys was trying to find a golf course to play on but wasn't having much luck. (They never played because they were too busy.) Emil complained about the mail service, *"Boy I'm just dying to get a letter from you."* The movie, "Sweet Rosie O'Grady" was playing. He saw "Thirty Seconds Over Tokyo" but didn't think much of it.

Emil had shore patrol duty for eight hours and was dead tired. That's how he got his cold—patrolling a bad section but he didn't have any trouble. He complained that he couldn't find a tailor to press his clothes, so he had to press his dress blues himself. He decided that he would do all the ironing when he got back.

"Flash! The mail just came in, and I received a total of one letter from you, dear, dated June 5th... Now I feel perfect, dear, just from reading your letter."

"Still Your Sweetie Pie"

Postmarked July 12, 1945: (Written July 8; Letter Twenty from the Murzim.)

"My Dearest Darlin',

Ellie must have guessed where Emil was, because he said, *"Yes dear, your guess was right. I had a feeling when we left the states that I would see that place... Australia."* Emil tried to get pictures taken while in port with no success but would keep trying. Something happened to Ellie's watch. Must have been the one Emil bought her for Christmas. Emil commented on her birthday celebrations that she must have described. She had an unusual birthday cake. She sent a family photo of the party and changed her hairstyle. Emil liked it. He mentioned that he worked until 8:30 Saturday night installing a new motor.

"Give my love to all, Sweet...

"Still Your Sweetie Pie"

Postmarked July 21, 1945: (Written July 20; Letter Twenty-one from the Murzim.)

"My Dearest Darlin',

"Gosh, sweet, your last letter dated July 13th arrived yesterday the 19th... that makes me feel good when I can get them so soon." The first-class electrician on board was sent home, because his time was up overseas, so now Emil was in charge. *"...so I pity the boys in the shop now, because I'm in charge now."* Emil got permission to take an unofficial course of the "Gyro Compass," which will help him aboard the ship, because he was in charge of maintaining the one on his ship. (He told me that every day for a few months he drove a jeep to town for the course and had to drive on the right side of the road.) Emil was upset. "Valley of Decision" was playing at one of the base theatres and they had an air raid about 15 minutes into the movie, so the showing was cancelled. *"Boy, was I mad after you writing me and telling how good it was,"* he complained to Ellie. He was listening to the "hit parade" on the radio while writing this letter, and he wrote that he didn't like the selections.

"Good night, Sweetheart. Still Your Sweetie Pie"

Postmarked August 3, 1945: (Written July 29; Letter Twenty-Two from the Murzim.)

"Hello Me Love—(He was trying out an Australian greeting.)

Emil had received a letter from a friend and learned that another friend's (Emil Clark) brother had died on Luzon. Emil

67

thought they were going to be on the move again. *"I think this trip will be pretty good duty, so don't worry, honey."*

Today was Sunday, and for the first time in six weeks they could take it easy. Emil was listening to "The Andrew Sisters' Show" on the radio. He mentioned he was in his fifteenth month of overseas duty. *"...so maybe it will only be a few months yet!!!"* He told Ellie how comfortable the moccasins she sent him were. *"Why it's almost like being at home sitting in a nice easy chair. Well I can dream, dear."* He saw the movie "It Happened Tomorrow" with Dick Powell and Linda Darnell, and "Wing and a Prayer" with Don Ameche and Dana Andrews.

"Still Your Sweetie Pie"

Postmarked August 10, 1945: (Written August 7; Letter Twenty-three from the Murzim.)

"My Dearest Darlin',

They had traveled to another port again, and the sea was smooth sailing for a change. *"I have an electric stricker in the shop now, so there are four of us, and I might possibly get another. Maybe I can take it easy then and just give orders! Ha! Ha!... The chow smells pretty good tonight, so I'll close now and see if it's as good as it smells."*

"Still Your Sweetie Pie"

Postmarked August 13: (Written August 11; Letter Twenty-four from the Murzim.)

"My Dearest Darlin',

Letters were coming in a timely fashion now. He received a letter from sister Tillie and a little gift enclosed from his mother. Sensing the end of the war was near, he writes, *"Well sweet, it's needless to ask you how your feelings are about the latest news. I myself am waiting for a definite confirmation before I start building up any hopes. Let's hope that my next letter to you will be the real thing. Boy, you should have seen the outburst we had here when it was first announced. Honey, I never knew an island out here could produce so many lights in such a short time."* Emil mentioned he felt lazy and worn out. He thought the heat was getting to him. He saw the movie, "Roughly Speaking." Said it was one of the best he had seen. Ellie still hadn't received the birthday gift he sent in June.

"Still Your Sweetie Pie"

Postmarked August 15: (Written August 14; Letter Twenty-five from the Murzim.)

"Hello My Darlin',

The radio was announcing an unconfirmed report of Japan's surrender. *"I sure hope it becomes a reality soon. Saw a terrible movie, "Manilla Calling... the next movie, "Here Come the Waves" should be better."* Emil kept busy repairing a wash machine on board by installing a new motor. They will pay some guys a slight sum to do the laundry. On another subject: *"Yes, sweet, I'm almost sure our children will have curly hair..."*

"Still Your Sweetie Pie"

JAPAN SURRENDERS...............JAPAN SURRENDERS!!!!!!!!!

Postmarked August 19, 1945: (Written August 17; Letter
Twenty-six from the Murzim.)

"My Dearest Darlin',

*"How's my honey feeling after listening to the end of the
war? What a silly question! Well, now comes the matter of my
getting out of the service... in today's news broadcast, it was
announced the Navy and Coast Guard have a point system
worked out, discharging men with 44 points or more... if I get
good breaks I might be able to get home in a couple of months,
my having 45 points... I know I shouldn't be building up hopes,
but that's the only thing I have to look forward to, my being
able to come home to you soon, sweet."*

Emil wrote that a fellow who lived in New Bavaria, Ohio,
was getting emergency leave because of his father's illness
and promised to stop and see Ellie. Emil sent a gift for her
with him. *"...everyone keeps their ears glued to the radio now
that it's over and everyone has one thing in mind. Give you
three guesses, Sweet. Ha!... I just finished taking a shower* (they
had salt-water showers) *and will be ready to eat... the pie
really looks good, but for the life of me, I can't figure out what
kind it's supposed to be. Well, I'll survive."*

"Still Your Sweetie Pie"

COMING HOME!!!!
DISCHARGE FROM US ARMY MANNING DETACHMENT
Navy 920
San Francisco

September 3, 1945:

"My Dearest Darlin',

"It's been quite a while since you've heard from me, but I know you realize something held my letter writing up and that something is really worthwhile. I had it all planned that when this time came I'd write a fancy letter to you, but now that it's come, all I'll say is I'm coming home for good, sweet. Yes, honey, right now I'm on, or should I say at, one of the DISCHARGE centers overseas, and as soon as transportation is available it will take about two weeks to reach the states. From there on in, it will be a matter of only a few days, and I'll be a FREE man, or whatever they want to call me.

"Well, now that I've given you the good news, sweet, don't write anymore, because I wouldn't receive it anyway. And please pass it on to the folks about my coming home and not writing, as if I have to tell you. As soon as I reach the states, I'll call you up, if possible, or wire you. O.K., honey?

"They're still censoring our mail, so that's about all I can write, except to tell you that it's finally happened.

"Boy, am I on air!

"Give my love to all and please take extra, extra good care of yourself.

"Still Your Sweetie Pie, Love Emil

"PS: I love you and will see you soon."

FROM NAVY REPLACEMENT CENTER, SAN FRANCISCO
September 12, 1945:

"My Dearest Darlin',

"Hello honey, are you getting prepared for my return? Ha! Ha! Hanging around shore station—one step closer to home... Gather my civilian clothes," were the instructions from Emil. *"...won't take me more than two minutes to get out of this uniform into good old civies."* The food had not been so hot.

There were too many men to feed at the shore station. Before he left the ship, Emil had received a package from Ellie sent in October, 1944 to the F-7 boat! *"Wonderful service, wasn't it!"* kidded Emil. It contained canned food (shrimp), writing paper gum and cough drops. The only thing he threw out was the cough drops. Surprisingly, everything else was okay. He especially enjoyed the canned shrimp.

"Thanks a million, honey." He mentioned that it had rained every night while at the holding station. He was going to throw his mattress and hammock away, but will keep three-quarters of his sea bag and ditty bag. He mentioned he wanted to take a week off and go on a second honeymoon when he got home, wherever Ellie wanted to go. (They went to Niagara Falls.)

"Just think, no more blue suits with thirteen buttons to hinder me. Ha! Ha!" Emil quipped. *"You know, sweet, I just can't express the happiness within me knowing that we'll be together for good always."* Emil promised to call or wire Ellie upon reaching the coast. *"I'll be seeing you soon."*

"Still Your Sweetie Pie"

Emil and his crew were actually at the holding station for six weeks, because there were so many soldiers coming home, that they didn't have enough trains to take them. So to pass the time, he and some of the guys volunteered to be lumberjacks.

Lumberjacking in New Guinea, November 1944 while awaiting new orders.

Last Letter from USCG Barracks, Paine Field, Everett, Washington:

October 30, 1945:

"My Dearest Darlin',

"Don't fall over, sweet. Yes, I'm actually writing. Conditions have been such that my intended letters would not have been enjoyable reading, so please forgive me, dear, for not writing sooner.

"Just a few minutes ago I was informed of my transfer date being set for Nov. 1st (Thursday) and if the train is not delayed, I should be in Detroit this coming Monday, at which place I'm to receive my discharge papers. According to this set-up, I should arrive in Cleveland either Thursday or Friday of next week, with no more strings attaching me to the service.

"Gosh, darling, it seems so hard to believe that we'll be together again and this time for GOOD. Honey, there's so much I want to thank you for, due to your thoughtfulness and consideration throughout the time that we've known and shared together, that I won't be able to express them in a million years.

"Well, sweet, you'll have my civilian clothes ready for me, won't you? As I mentioned a while back, it won't take me but two minutes to get into them. By the way, honey, as soon as possible upon arriving in Detroit I'll send a wire letting you know the exact time I'll arrive in Cleveland.

"I've been stationed in three different ports of the state of Washington, and at last they've given me the date of my departure. Boy, I thought I'd never get away from here.

"Well, sweetheart, until I arrive in Detroit, you won't hear from me, so give my love to all, and please take the very, very best care of yourself.

"Still Your Sweetie Pie, Love Emil

"P.S. It won't be long now, 'Funny Face.'"

73

EMIL FINALLY ARRIVED HOME ON November 7, 1945!!!

When I asked him how he felt upon returning, Emil commented in 2010 at the age of ninety years old, *"I was gladder than
hell, and relieved!!!!"*

Emil Rupert Takacs
Apprentice Seaman
Enlisted December 8, 1941

Note from his father, Rupert Takacs, on back of photo

Translation:

I'm sending you a picture and keeping one and enjoying it. Rose, my dear daughter, I have been sick for eight years and can't travel to visit.

I send my love and will love you all until the day I die.

Please write to me and let me know how you are doing. I wish you good health.

59 Hazelwood Ave., Pittsburgh PA

Rupert Takacs

Emil—Apprentice Seaman   1942   Seaman First Class

Emil and brother-in-law Carl

Emil and brother Bill, 1942.

Emil's brother Bill, Ohio National Guard, 1942.

Chippewa Lake, Ohio
"The Cottage" 1940's

L-R Top: Bill Takacs & girlfriend Tillie Lukcso, Ellie and Emil (with pipe).
Bottom L-R: Andy Lukcso, Rose Gedeon holding Barbara Lukcso, Doris Gedeon, Rosemarie Gedeon.

Top row L-R: Andy, Barbie, Tillie Lukcso, Bill Takacs, Carl Gedeon.
Bottom L-R: Doris Gedeon, Ellie Takacs, Rosemarie Gedeon.

L-R: Rose Gedeon, Emil and Ellie Takacs

Playing in the Haystack: Rose Gedeon on top of ladder with Ellie Takacs behind.

L-R: Rosemarie, Emil Doris, 1943.

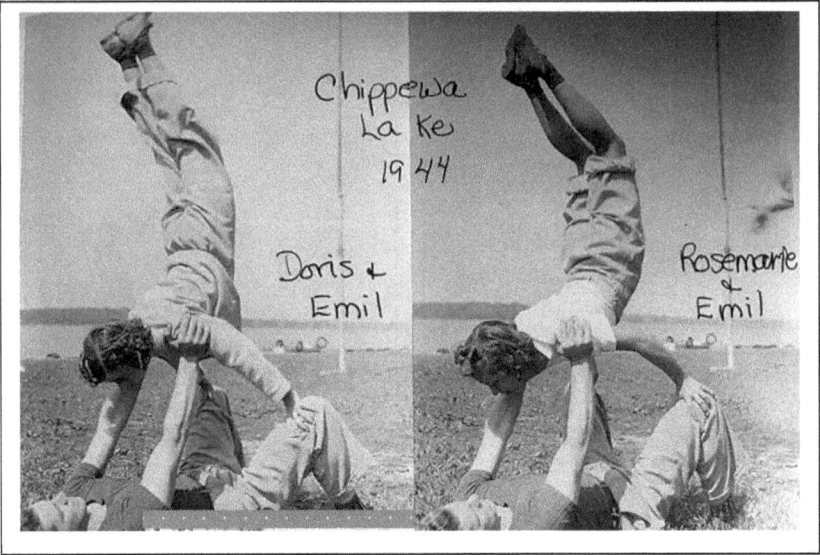

Chippewa
Lake
1944

Doris &
Emil

Rosemarie
&
Emil

| Doris | Rose | Ellie |
| Gedeon | Gedeon | Takacs |

Doris 12th birthday party Nov. 9, 1944
Tillie, Ellie, Rose, Edesyanam, Florence (friend),
Barbara, Doris

1942: Doris, Tillie, Bill, Ellie, Barbara, 1935 Ford.

Emil's mother, Gizella Takacs.
We call her "Edesyanam"
(Sweet Mother in Hungarian.)

L-R: Barbie Lukcso, Rosemarie
Gedeon, Doris Gedeon, Ellie
Takacs.

Epilogue

One can only imagine the long-anticipated reunion and homecoming that Emil and Ellie had after four, long years of uncertainty during WWII. Apparently it was an amorous reunion, because their first daughter, Adele Jean (me), was born EXACTLY nine months to the day, after his return. Emil returned on November 7, 1945, and Adele was born on August 7, 1946! And sister Donna Lee, followed four-and-one-half years later, when she was born on March 19, 1951, in a big snowstorm. Emil said the car got stuck in the driveway, and they had to call a paddy wagon to take Ellie to the hospital. She was so embarrassed. (That would be Mom!)

Emil and Ellie enjoyed 55 years together. They lived 28 years of their marriage, from 1950-1979, in Brooklyn Heights, Ohio, where they raised their family. Then they retired to Florida, living in Cooper City and Boynton Beach from 1979-2007.

Ellie passed away at the age of 78 in 1998, with Emil and Adele and Donna by her side. Emil lived in Florida alone for nine years, until cancer brought him to Columbus, Ohio, where he resided at Welsey Ridge Assisted Living until his death at age 91, in 2010. Appropriately, the date was June 6, which was the anniversary of D-Day during WWII.

Adele and Donna are eternally grateful for that chance meeting on the streetcar. *God knew what he was doing!*

Ellie and Emil Takacs, pregnant with Adele in April 1946. Adele Jean Takacs was born August 7, 1946, exactly nine months to the day that Emil came home from the war, November 7, 1945!

The Journey

The writing of this book was a journey of 17 years —
from 2000 when Emil gave the letters to Adele, until 2017
upon its completion.

Writing is done in spurts and starts, while raising my
family and caring for grandchildren. It was one of those
grandchildren who reignited my interest. When Jenna was
about eight years old, she found the letters in a fireproof box
under a bed upstairs. She asked what was in the box, and as I
showed her, she was fascinated by the thin, air-mail paper,
and she wanted me to read a letter to her.

While Emil's handwriting was beautiful, it was difficult
for a child to decipher. So I began to write again. And five
years later when Jenna was 13, she did a Veteran's Day
project and used information from my book. That was in
2017. I have included her report and photos of her in her
great-grandpa's Coast Guard uniforms. So Thank You, Jenna,
for your interest in our family history.

I also must thank my sister and our cousins who have
encouraged me along the way. Their notes of appreciation
have meant a lot to me and kept me writing!

I am grateful to have finished this story, but also a little
sad because this journey has kept me close to Mom and Dad,
just imagining what those years were like for them. So it is
with bittersweet emotion that I end this Love Story and
profound gratefulness that it happened!

Adele Takacs Johnston

Related Stories

My sister and her husband, Karl, visited Boston in 2013. Donna posed in front of the same statue that our dad stood in front of in the Boston Commons. And they found the same row-house that our parents rented while Dad was attending electrician school at Franklin Institute. We knew the address because they had saved the application form for their ration book, which had their Boston address ad 428 Marlborough St., Boston, Massachusetts!

So Donna also posed on the steps of the house in the rain. On their next trip to Boston, Donna and Karl will try to find Franklin Institute. There's a photo of Dad's class at Franklin earlier in the book.

Beginning and End of the War

In the process of writing the book, I asked Dad in a phone conversation how he felt when the announcement came that the war was over. His response: *"I wondered what I was doing here."*

And when I asked him how he felt when the Japanese bombed Pearl Harbor on December 7, 1941, he said he was angry and thought, *"How dare they bomb us when the Japanese ambassador was in the United States for peace talks!"*

He was working 16-hour days at Alcoa, Monday through Friday, and Saturday and Sunday were eight-hour days at the time.

The very next day he enlisted in the Coast Guard.

Alex Haley
Coast Guard, USS Murzim

Dad told me that "Roots" author, Alex Haley, was on the Murzim at the same time he was. Alex was a cook on the ship and used to write letters to the guys' sweet-hearts for $1 per letter. It wasn't until Dad watched the made-for-TV movie, "Roots," and saw the ship's life preserver with the USS Murzim written on it that he realized it was the very same Alex Haley with whom he'd served!

Knowing this, I did more research on Alex, and I discovered the following information.

In a Reader's Digest article, written in 1961, it stated that Alex Haley enlisted in the Coast Guard when he was 17 years old as a mess boy. He composed love letters for his buddies, which they sent to wives and sweethearts. An illiterate first-class steward's mate set Haley to writing love letters for fellow blacks on the mess deck. After the war, Haley continued to write and became the Coast Guard's first Chief Journalist.

On Tthanksgiving Day, November 24th, a famous article he wrote was posted. Here are some excerpts that will give you an idea of life on the Murzim:

"It was 1943, during World War II, and I was a young US Coastguardsman. My ship, the USS Murzim, had been under way for days. Most of her holds contained thousands of cartons of canned or dried foods. The other holds were loaded with five-hundred-pound bombs, packed delicately in padded racks. Our destination was a big base on the island of Tulagi, in the South Pacific...

"We unloaded cargo, reloaded with something else, then again we put to sea in the routine familiar to us, and as the days became weeks, my little person experience receded.

"Sometimes when we were at sea, a mail ship would rendezvous and bring us mail from home, which, of course, we accorded topmost priority.

"Every time the ship's loudspeaker rasped, 'Attention! Mail Call!' two-hundred-odd shipmates came pounding up on deck and clustered about the two seamen standing by those precious, bulging, gray sacks. They were alternately pulling out fistfuls of letters and barking successive names of sailors who were, in turn, shouting back 'Here! Here!' amid the pushing.

"Now approaching another Thanksgiving, I have asked myself what will I wish for all who are reading this, for our nation, indeed for our whole world—since, quoting a good and wise friend of mine, 'In the end we are mightily and merely people, each with similar needs.' First I wish for us, of course, the simple, common sense to achieve world peace, that being paramount for the very survival of our kind."

An impressive footnote is that Alex Haley had imprinted across the bottom of his stationery:
"Find the good—and praise..."

Cousins' Memories of WWII

In 2002, I asked Rosie(Gedeon) Owens and Doris (Gedeon) May for some of their memories of Emil and Ellie before and during the war years. Both of them thought of Emil as their older brother, because, according to Rosie, "We all lived in one house on W. 129th Street. Aunt Tillie, Uncle Bill, Emil, Mom (Rose Gedeon), Dad (Carl Gedeon), Edesyanam (Gizella Takacs), Rosie and Dorie. Grandma Gedeon at one point also lived with us—just one, BIG happy family!"

Rosie also recalled riding in Emil's little red wagon and

helping him deliver newspapers at ½ cent per paper Once he was supposed to be watching her, but he got involved in a baseball game, and Rosie wandered away. "I don't think he babysat me after that," commented Rosie.

Both Dorie and Rosie remembered getting bags of candy with prizes every Saturday at the Variety Theatre, where Emil was head usher. "Emil always made sure we got the prize bag," they recalled.

And both remembered the wonderful times at Chippewa Lake. Dorie wrote, "I can remember best the times we had at Chippewa Lake Cottage when I was seven or eight years old. Because of the war, we never went anywhere on vacation, so we enjoyed one month out there being on the beach and at the amusement park. Your mom (Ellie) worked, but did seem to come out when we could have a good amount of time with her. Barb was about two and was the big attraction. Because your dad (Emil) was in the service, it gave her a place to come on vacation. After Andy and Carl came along, they decided to sell the cottage. I was eleven by then, and we did have four good years of vacationing."

Dorie was nine when she remembered Emil coming into Aunt Tillie's kitchen and announcing he had just joined the Coast Guard and would be in for four years. He joined on December 8, 1941, the day after the Japanese bombed Pearl Harbor, December 7, 1941.

"We were all shocked, and so was your mother (Ellie)!" Dorie wrote letters and sent pictures to Emil. She was a teenager when he came home after the war. While Emil was in the service, Dorie's mom (Rose Gedeon) would go with Ellie to visit Emil while he was stationed in Chicago.

"It was a long four years, but when your dad came home, he made up for lost time, and you (Adele) were born nine months later. He has always been a wonderful uncle to me."

Thank you, Rosie and Dorie, for your wonderful memories that our family can treasure!

Dear Adele,

What a tribute to your mom and dad. You did a terrific job. I especially liked the Chippewa Lake part, as I spent my summers there as a kid. I just found out my girlfriend's sister lived there year-around for ten years, during her grade-school years. The ironic part was the house her mom had built was also on Playland Parkway, the same street we lived on. Small World!

P.S. I found a couple of pictures of the old Cottage, called the "Truck Inn" named after Uncle A's trucking business. Many a good time was had here.

Thank you for sending me the Love  Story, which I was a part of!

Love Rosie,

Random Stories

During the process of writing this Love Story, I was fortunate enough to have my dad to help. In the summers when he would visit Ohio, we would go over each letter, and he would answer questions and embellish in certain areas. He also added random stories in the course of our conversations. So here are a few stories about a clock, his father, Rupert Takacs, Chippewa Lake, and Uncle Carl Gedeon.

The Clock

Emil was seven in 1926. The mantel clock was not working, so he decided to take it apart and try to fix it. He put it back together and hid it under his parents' bed. At 2 a.m., the clock decided to work and bonged loudly! It woke up the household. Emil confessed to his crime and was punished.

Rupert Takacs

Emil remembers his parents fighting a lot. One day, again when he was seven, he came home for lunch and was sitting on the porch steps when his father brought him a pair of shoes (that were too small), and he never saw his father again. He left his family and started a new one with someone else.

Emil was bitter that he didn't have his father. But when the family went to live with married sister, Rose and her husband, Carl, dear Uncle Carl became Emil's father figure.

Chippewa Lake

In the late 1930's, before Emil joined the Coast Guard, he worked at the Variety Theatre. He and his buddies would load up into a car after they closed up at 10 p.m., and drive out Pearl Road to Chippewa Lake, where his sisters owned a cottage. The guys arrived at midnight— often running out of gas along the way. Gas was 25 cents a gallon then. They played cards until 4 a.m., and then at 6 a.m., the girls next door came over to play tennis. At 3:30 in the afternoon, they headed back to Cleveland to work at the theatre that night. They only had two hours sleep! The amazing part, Emil recalls, is that they all survived!

Uncle Carl and the Move

In 1951, six months after Donna was born in that snowstorm, Emil moved his family to Brooklyn Heights in a rainstorm. Uncle Carl and Al and Rosie Owens helped them. There were no paved streets, so the 1947 black Plymouth got stuck in a ditch. Emil told Carl to push behind, and Emil gunned the car, and Carl got covered in mud! Lots of laughs over that one!

Time Line

1. December 8, 1940—Enlisted in the Coast Guard the day after Pearl Harbor was bombed by the Japanese.
2. December 18, 1941—St. Louis, Missouri.
3. December 29, 1941—New Orleans, LA (Algiers) basic training boot camp.
4. January-April, 1942—Chicago, IL (Help new recruits).
5. June-September, 1942—Great Lakes, Smith Thompson ore ship.
6. August, 1942—Seneca, IL, La Salle Hotel and Chicago, IL, Hotel Berkshire.
7. September, 1942—Boat patrol protecting Great Lakes.
8. February, 1943—Chicago stockyards.
9. April 3, 1943—Married Eldrid June Takacs at the Old Stone Church, Cleveland, OH.
10. May-August, 1943—Lived together in Boston MA, while attending Franklin Institute of Technology (electrician school); graduated Petty Officer 3rd Class.
11. September 4, 1943—San Francisco, CA.
12. September 22, 1943—Reassigned to Great Lakes Life Boat Station in Michigan, IN.
13. November 8, 1943—Great Lakes Training Station in Illinois for anti-aircraft gun training.
14. December, 1943—Patrol Great Lakes for missing aircraft.
15. February-April 1944—Coast Guard Station in Ludington, MI; Ellie lived in Michigan City with Emil.
16. April 30, 1944—Barstow, CA.

17. May 2, 1944—Alameda, CA.

18. May 25, 1944—Wilmington, CA (receiving station).

19. June-August, 1944—F-7 transport ship took three months to travel the South Pacific, stopping at the Hawaiian and Marshall Islands, etc.

20. September 9, 1944-January, 1945—New Guinea; transported ammunition to surrounding islands, the Guada Canal and the Philippines.

21. October 29, 1944—Leyte Gulf battle, and was awarded the Bronze Cluster medal.

22. November 27, 1944—Enemy air attack.

23. January 26-August 19, 1945—Aboard ammunition ship USS Murzim.

24. June1, 1945—USS Murzim in Brisbane, Australia port.

25. August, 1945—Japan surrenders!

26. September, 1945—San Francisco, CA, Honorably discharged from the US Coast Guard as Petty Officer 2nd Class (electrician).

27. October, 1945—USCG Barracks, Paine Field, Everett, WA.

28 November 7, 1945—HOME (via train to Detroit, MI and then to Cleveland, OH).

Emil Rupert Takacs

Served in the U.S. Coast Guard December 8, 1941-November 7, 1945.

Honorably Discharged as Petty Officer 2nd Class, electrician.

Earned Bronze Cluster in the Battle of Leyte.

Last assignment aboard the U.S.S. Murzim, AK95.

Star Essay

November 6, 2014
Veteran's Day Project
Jenna Suhy

My great grandpa, Emil Rupert Takacs (my grandma's dad), enlisted in the Coast Guard December 8th, 1941, the day after the Japanese bombed Pearl Harbor in World War II. He decided on the Coast Guard because he didn't want to be in the infantry, and he heard the Coast Guard served better food. Ten days after he enlisted he was deployed to St. Louis, Missouri. After that he went to boot camp in Algiers, Louisiana. Then he went to Chicago, Illinois for more training and was stationed on the Great Lakes from June 1st, 1942 to March 30th, 1943. He was on the Smith Thompson Ore ship picking up ore in Lake Superior ports and unloading it in Lake Erie ports.

He was married to Eldrid June Lohman on April 3rd, 1943 at The Old Stone Church in Cleveland, Ohio. Together they went to Boston for training at Franklin Institute electrician school and lived there for four months. In September of 1943, he went to San Francisco and was reassigned to the Great Lakes Lifeboat Station. In November of 1943, he went to the Great Lakes Training Station in Illinois for anti-aircraft gun training. Then he was sent to Barstow, CA and was ordered to go overseas on transport ship to the South Pacific. He was assigned to an army transport ship in May of 1944. There were 33 transport ships sent to Honolulu and only 11 made it. It took them two months to travel, and my grandpa's boat was one of the 11 that made it. The transport ship then went to New Guinea where he was assigned to the ammunition ship U.S.S. Murzim in September of 1944. He was the electrician on the ship, which delivered ammunition to the U.S. ports in the South Pacific. He was on the ship for 18 months and discharged from the service after the war was over on November 7th, 1945.

My Great Grandma and Grandpa Takacs went on to enjoy 55 years of marriage.

Jenna modeling her great-grandpa's dress blues and working white Coast Guards uniforms.

The next generation carries on...

www.ingramcontent.com/pod-product-compliance
Lightning Source LLC
Chambersburg PA
CBHW061753020426
42331CB00006B/1463